HiPPoS CAN'T SWiM

and other fun facts

For John Daniel
—L. D.

For M & D
—H. E.

To Vincent and William,
for the constant inspiration and interruption.
Love, Dad
—P. O.

LITTLE SIMON
An imprint of Simon & Schuster Children's Publishing Division
1230 Avenue of the Americas, New York, New York 10020
Series concept by Laura Lyn DiSiena
Copyright © 2014 by Simon & Schuster, Inc.
All rights reserved, including the right of reproduction in whole or in part in any form.
LITTLE SIMON is a registered trademark of Simon & Schuster, Inc., and associated colophon is a trademark of Simon & Schuster, Inc.
For information about special discounts for bulk purchases, please contact Simon & Schuster Special Sales at 1-866-506-1949 or business@simonandschuster.com.
The Simon & Schuster Speakers Bureau can bring authors to your live event. For more information or to book an event contact the
Simon & Schuster Speakers Bureau at 1-866-248-3049 or visit our website at www.simonspeakers.com.
Manufactured in China 1022 SCP
10 9
DiSiena, Laura Lyn. Hippos can't swim : and other fun facts / by Laura Lyn DiSiena and Hannah
Eliot ; illustrated by Pete Oswald. — 1st ed. p. cm. — (Did you know?)
Summary: "A book of fun facts about animals of all sizes, shapes, and species!"-- Provided by publisher. Audience: 4-8. Audience: K to grade 3. Includes bibliographical references and index.
ISBN 978-1-4424-9324-7 (pbk : alk. paper) — ISBN 978-1-4424-9352-0 (hc :alk. paper) — ISBN 978-1-4424-9325-4 (ebook : alk. paper) 1. Hippopotamidae—Miscellanea--Juvenile literature.
2. Animals—Miscellanea—Juvenile literature. 3. Children's questions and answers. I. Eliot, Hannah. II. Oswald, Pete, ill. III. Title. IV. Title: Hippos can not swim.
QL737.U57D57 2014   590.2—dc23   2013009391

DID YOU KNOW?

HIPPOS CAN'T SWIM

and other fun facts

By Laura Lyn DiSiena and Hannah Eliot

Illustrated by Pete Oswald

LITTLE SIMON

New York   London   Toronto   Sydney   New Delhi

HEY THERE!

Did you know that hippos are the third-largest living land mammals? They come right after elephants and white rhinos!

2nd

1st

3rd

Did you know that a hippo's nose, ears, and eyes are all on the top of its head? That way a hippo can still breathe, hear, and see while the rest of it is underwater!

OKAY, OKAY.
MAYBE YOU KNEW ALL THAT.

But did you know that hippos can't SWIM?
That's right! Their bodies are too dense to float.
Instead, hippos walk underwater along the riverbed
or use their feet to push off it in order to move!

SPLISH! SPLASH!

Can you swim? If you ever go swimming in an ocean, there's a chance you'll run into a sea turtle. Even though sea turtles seem like slow animals, they can swim up to 35 miles per hour!

That's much faster than lots of other sea creatures can go, and much, MUCH faster than a jellyfish can move.

Jellyfish float with the currents of the ocean. Wouldn't it be nice to float all day long?

Some jellyfish can produce light in their bodies.

This is called BioLUMINESCENCE.

Jellyfish use this quality to scare off predators since the light can startle other animals.

Fireflies glow too. But they use their glow to communicate with other fireflies and to attract a mate. They can control their glow so that it stays steady, pulses, or flashes every so often.

A firefly's light comes in different colors.
It can be green, yellow, or even red!

Zebras don't come in lots of different colors, but their black-and-white stripes do help camouflage them. To predators such as lions, the stripes appear to blend in to the wavy African grass!

Did you know that a zebra's stripes are as unique as a human's fingerprints? Zebras may all *seem* the same, but no two zebras look alike—just like no two *humans* look alike!

Zebras are attracted to things that are black-and-white striped—just like they are. If you simply painted black-and-white stripes on a wall, a zebra would walk toward it.

Raccoons, on the other hand, are attracted to shiny objects like aluminum foil, pots, pans, and . . .

RUStle!
RUStle!

Look out for the furry animals in your garbage cans!

Chipmunks are more likely to be found in the woods than in your garbage can. Did you know that all summer long they collect nuts, seeds, and berries by stuffing them in their cheeks? Then they drop off the food at their homes.

When the chipmunks return home to hibernate for the winter, they slowly eat all the food they collected in their cheek pouches over the summer!

BOING!

Kangaroos have pouches too, but kangaroos are marsupials. This means that their pouches are used to carry their babies.

BOING!

As you probably know, kangaroos hop everywhere. They use their strong back legs to hop, and their muscular tails for balance. If you bounce on a pogo stick, you can hop like a kangaroo too!

A rabbit is another animal that hops. Rabbits may hop much more slowly than kangaroos, but the longest rabbit hop ever recorded is almost 10 feet!

Rabbits can give birth to up to 35 little baby bunnies per year. Some types of rabbits live as families in underground burrows. It's nice and cozy down there.

Some bats also live underground in caves.
Others live aboveground in trees.

Bats have excellent hearing. If there is an object or animal nearby, a bat will send out a sound that bounces off the object, and then echoes back to the bat. By doing this, a bat can figure out how big the object is, how far away it is, and how fast it's traveling.

747 airplane, traveling at 547 miles per hour, 2 miles away.

COOL! CAN YOU DO THAT?

While bats sleep all day, worker ants in a colony don't sleep all day *or* all night. Instead, they each take about 250 naps throughout the day, each nap lasting just longer than a minute. This way, many of the ants are awake at one time and can continue building the colony.

Did you know that great blue herons live in colonies as well?
They mostly live along coastlines or near ponds or streams.

Herons catch fish by standing still for long periods of time and waiting for the fish to swim by. That may sound boring to you, but herons do it to survive!

Herons are 3-feet to 5-feet tall on average, whereas hummingbirds are among the smallest of birds! They are usually only about 3-*inches* to 5-inches tall. They're so tiny that sometimes they look like flying insects.

Hummmmmmmmm!

Hummingbirds can hover in midair by rapidly flapping their wings 12 to 80 times per second!

Blue whales are bigger than both hummingbirds and herons. They're actually the largest animals that have ever lived.

DID YOU KNOW THAT?

They can grow up to 100-feet long and weigh up to 180 tons!

And unlike hippos . . .
blue whales sure can

SWIM!

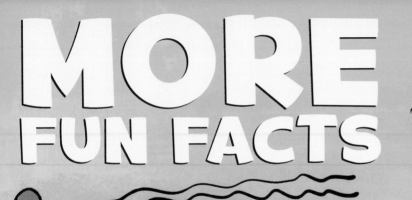

MORE FUN FACTS

Hippopotamus: The word "hippopotamus" comes from the ancient Greek word for "river horse." But hippos are not related to horses at all. They most closely resemble pigs, whales, and dolphins!

Sea turtle: The average life span of sea turtles is more than 50 years! That's a long time for an animal.

Jellyfish: The biggest known jellyfish is the Arctic lion's mane, whose tentacles can extend up to 120 feet.

Firefly: Baby fireflies are called larvae. They live underground and feed on worms and slugs by injecting them with a numbing fluid.

Zebra: Zebras are constantly looking for fresh grass and water. Sometimes they gather in herds of thousands to find food. And they often travel with other animals, such as wildebeest.

Raccoon: When it comes to heights, raccoons have no fear. They scamper up trees to get away from predators.

Kangaroo: Kangaroos have some funny names! Females are called "flyers," "jills," or "does." Males are called "bucks," "boomers," or "old men." And young kangaroos are called "joeys."

Chipmunk: Chipmunks "chirp" when they sense a threat.

chirp!

Rabbit: Rabbit mothers typically only feed their babies for a few minutes a day.

Joey

Hummingbird: Hummingbirds can fly backward and even upside down!

Bat: Bats are very clean animals! Like cats, they groom themselves all day to keep their fur soft and clean.

Great blue heron: Thanks to specially shaped vertebrae, herons can curl their necks into an S shape, which allows them to fly faster and to catch fish more easily.

zzz

Blue whale: Blue whales can rest easy. They are so large that they have very few known predators.

Ant: Ants can lift anywhere from 10 to 50 times their own body weight!